VOLUME 4

I0541470

She

delighting in the examples
of the women of the Bible

Delight Thyself
DESIGN MINISTRIES

delightthyself.com

Copyright © 2023 by Delight Thyself Design Ministries, Inc.

All Scripture quotations are taken from the King James Bible.

Published by Delight In Him Publications,
a division of Delight Thyself Design Ministries in Hurricane, WV.

The mission of Delight Thyself Design Ministries is to design and distribute the printed Word of the Gospel of Jesus Christ.

All rights reserved. No part of this book may be reproduced or transmitted in any form or by any means electronic, mechanical, photocopy, recording, or otherwise without the written permission of the publisher, except for brief quotations in online or printed reviews.

Delight Thyself Design Ministries, Inc.
PO Box 725
Hurricane, WV 25526
delightthyself.com

The contents of this book are the result of years of spiritual growth in life and ministry. Every effort has been made to give proper credit and attribution to quotes and information that is not original. It is not our intent to claim originality with any quote or thought that could not be tied to an original source.

Special thanks to Erika Daniel & Madyson Davis for helping finish the layout.

Printed in the United States of America.

ISBN: 979-8-9897788-0-5

To each of the Godly ladies
who have pointed me to His Word.

Psalm 28:7
"The LORD is my strength and my shield; my heart trusted in him,
and I am helped: therefore my heart greatly rejoiceth..."

Also Available

Delight Thyself Also In The Lord:
a simple daily devotional

Delight Thyself Also In The Lord:
a simple daily devotional - Volume 2

Order My Steps In Thy Word:
a verse by verse study of Psalm 119

She:
Delighting In The Examples Of The Women Of The Bible

Volume 1	Volume 2
Abigail	Anna
Bathsheba	Eve
Deborah	Hannah
Lydia	Jochebed
Martha	Mary Magdalene
Mary Of Bethany	Naomi
Michal	Pharaoh's Daughter
Phebe	Ruth
The Syrophenician Woman	Sapphira
The Virtuous Woman	The True Harlot Mother
The Widow Of Zarephath	The Widow With Two Mites
The Woman In The City	The Woman With An Issue Of Blood

Volume 3
Elisabeth
Gomer
Leah
Mary The Mother Of Jesus
Rachel
Rahab
Rhoda
Tabitha
Tamar
The Shunammite Woman
The Widow Of Nain
The Woman In Adultery

VOLUME 4

The Women of the Bible

She...

The series of *She* consists of four volumes, each focusing on the lives of 12 women of the Bible. Many of the women are familiar, some less spoken of, but each are applicable to our lives today.

The objective of this series is not an effort to reveal some new theory about the women, but simply to point us to the pages of the Word of God so that the Lord can speak to us as only He can. Ask Him to show you the Truths found within the testimonies of each of these women that He has preserved for us to read.

Symbols:

The leaves around a name signify the beginning of the study of a new woman.

SHE...
This shows us a quality that we can apply to ourselves, or seek to become.

SHE...
This denotes a fact about them as women during their time in history.

Read

A suggested passage for the context of the study.

Memorize

Verse(s) to help apply the characteristics of the woman.

Apply

A question or two to encourage you to dwell on what can be learned from the example of the woman of the Bible.

Delilah

Judges 16:19

"...she caused him to shave off the seven locks of his head;"

SHE HAS BEEN CALLED THE JUDAS OF THE OLD TESTAMENT.

Judges 16:4-5

"And it came to pass afterward, that he _____ a woman in the valley of Sorek, whose name was Delilah. And the lords of the Philistines came up unto her, and said unto her, _____ him, and see wherein his great _____ lieth, and by what means we may _____ against him, that we may bind him to afflict him: and we will give thee every one of us _____ hundred pieces of silver."

She sold out Samson for at least 1,100 pieces of silver;
yet another picture that money is the root of all evil.

SHE BROUGHT WEAKNESS TO A MAN OF GREAT STRENGTH.

His love for her made him willing to give her anything she desired,
and she used that strength against him.

He told her three lies about the source of his strength.

SHE WAS PERSISTENT IN HER EVIL PLOT TO REMOVE HIS STRENGTH.

She urged him daily until he gave in to her tenacious requests.
Judges 16:16-17

SHE PERSUADED SAMSON TO TELL HER ALL OF HIS HEART.

Judges 16:18

"And when Delilah saw that he had told her _____ his heart, she sent and called for the lords of the Philistines, saying, _____ up this once, for he hath _____ me all his heart. Then the lords of the Philistines came up unto her, and brought _____ in their hand."

She sold her knowledge to the Philistines. Instead of stopping there, she allowed her sin to take her farther and farther until her mission was complete.

Judges 16:19

"And she made him _____ upon her knees; and she called for a man,

and she caused him to _____ off the seven locks of his head;

and she began to _____ him, and his _____ went from him."

She...

DELILAH SERVES AS AN EXAMPLE OF HOW SIN AND LUST CAN RUIN OUR REPUTATION.

Still today, very few women share her name. **Her lack of character is enshrined within the pages of Scripture for each generation to learn from her wickedness.**

Memorize:

1 Corinthians 10:6
"Now these things were our examples, to the intent we should not lust after evil things, as they also lusted."

Apply:

How is Delilah's deception an example to you?

_____

_____

Who is another example in the Bible of how sin and lust can ruin a reputation?

_____

Notes

_____

_____

_____

_____

_____

_____

_____

_____

_____

_____

_____

Esther

Esther

Esther 2:7

"...she had neither father nor mother..."

SHE WAS ALSO KNOWN AS HADADDAH.

Esther 2:7

"And he brought up _____, that is, Esther, his uncle's daughter: for she had

neither father nor mother, and the maid was _____ and _____; whom

Mordecai, when her father and mother were dead, took for his _____ daughter."

Her uncle, Mordecai, raised her after her parents died.
When the king appointed his officers to gather together the fair
young virgins of the kingdom, Mordecai brought her up to the palace.

Esther 2:9

"And the maiden pleased him, and she obtained _____ of him; and he speedily

gave her her _____ for purification, with such things as belonged to her, and seven

maidens, which were meet to be given her, out of the king's house: and he _____

her and her maids unto the _____ place of the house of the women."

Many maidens were brought before King Ahasuerus,
yet it was Esther who pleased him.

**God had ordered her footsteps and placed her exactly where she was
for a specific reason, exactly when she needed to be there.**

SHE HAD NOT YET SHOWN OR TOLD THAT SHE WAS A JEW.

Esther 2:10-11

"Esther had not shewed her _____ nor her _____: for Mordecai had charged

her that she should not shew it. And Mordecai walked _____ day before the court of

the women's house, to know how _____ did, and what should _____ of her."

She...

ESTHER SERVES AS AN EXAMPLE TO US
THAT GOD WILL DIRECT OUR STEPS
AND USE US ACCORDING TO HIS PURPOSE
IF ONLY WE WILL SURRENDER OUR LIVES TO HIM.

Memorize:

Psalm 37:23
"The steps of a good man are ordered by the LORD:
and he delighteth in his way."

Apply:

Write down a time when it was clear that the Lord ordered your steps:

_____

_____

_____

Esther 2:17

"...she obtained grace and favour in his sight..."

SHE REQUIRED NOTHING WHEN IT WAS HER TURN TO GO UNTO THE KING.

Esther 2:15

"Now when the turn of Esther, the daughter of _____ the uncle of _____, who had taken her for his daughter, was come to go in unto the king, she required _____ but what Hegai the king's chamberlain, the keeper of the women, _____. And Esther obtained favour in the sight of all them that looked upon her."

The king loved her more than all of the other women.
So much so that she obtained grace and favour in his sight.

SHE RECEIVED THE ROYAL CROWN WHICH MADE HER QUEEN.

Esther 2:17

"And the king _____ Esther above all the women, and she obtained grace and favour in his sight _____ than all the virgins; so that he set the royal _____ upon her head, and made her _____ instead of Vashti."

SHE WAS OBEDIENT.

SHE STILL HAD NOT REVEALED THAT SHE WAS A JEW, JUST AS MORDECAI HAD ADVISED.

Esther 2:20

"Esther had not yet shewed her _____ nor her _____; as Mordecai had charged her: for Esther did the _____ of Mordecai, like as when she was _____ up with him."

She...

ESTHER ALSO SERVES AS AN EXAMPLE THAT WE ARE ABLE TO OBTAIN GRACE AND FAVOUR IN THE SIGHT OF OUR KING.

HE WILL PROMOTE US ALSO,
IF ONLY WE ARE WILLING AND OBEDIENT UNTO HIM.

Memorize:

Psalm 75:6-7
"For promotion cometh neither from the east, nor from the west, nor from the south. But God is the judge: he putteth down one, and setteth up another."

Apply:

Why did Esther obtain grace and favour?

_____

_____

_____

"...she should go in unto the king..."

SHE WAS PLACED THERE AT A SPECIFIC TIME FOR A SPECIFIC PURPOSE.

Esther 4:8

"Also he gave him the copy of the writing of the _____ that was given at Shushan

to _____ them, to shew it unto Esther, and to declare it unto her,

and to _____ her that she should go in unto the king,

to make _____ unto him, and to make _____ before him for her people."

God creates divine appointments.
Where you are right now is for a purpose.

There was a law that if someone came unto the king without being called,
they could be put to death if the king did not hold out the golden sceptre.
Mordecai reminded Esther that she was there for a reason.

Esther 4:14

"For if thou altogether holdest thy _____ at this _____, then shall there

enlargement and deliverance _____ to the Jews from _____ place;

but thou and thy father's house shall be destroyed: and _____ knoweth whether

thou art come to the kingdom for _____ a time as _____?"

SHE ASKED HER PEOPLE TO FAST AND PRAY FOR HER.
Esther 4:16

"Go, gather together all of the _____ that are present in Shushan,

and _____ ye for me, and neither eat nor drink _____ days, night or day:

I also and my maidens will fast likewise; and so will I _____ in unto the king,

which is not according to the law: and if I _____, I perish."

SHE WAS BRAVE.

Esther 4:16

"...and if I _____, I perish."

She was even willing to die if that was the will of God.

SHE WAS USED OF GOD TO SAVE HER AND HIS PEOPLE.

 *She...*

ESTHER IS ALSO AN EXAMPLE OF HOW GOD CAN EMPOWER US TO DO GREAT THINGS FOR HIS GLORY.

Memorize:

Esther 4:14b
"...and who knoweth whether thou art come to the kingdom for such a time as this?"

Apply:

What would have happened to Esther if the king had not held out the golden sceptre?

_____

Would you be brave enough to risk your life for God's glory?

_____

Notes

_____

_____

_____

_____

_____

_____

_____

_____

_____

_____

_____

Hagar

Hagar

"...she fled from her face."

SHE WAS THE HANDMAID OF SARAI.

Genesis 16:1

"Now Sarai _____'s wife bare him no children:

and she had an _____, an Egyptian, whose name was Hagar."

SHE FLED FROM THE FACE OF SARAI, THE WIFE OF ABRAM.

He was the father of her son.
Sarai had told her husband to go in unto her,
and then delivered her unto him.

Genesis 16:3-4

"And Sarai Abram's wife took Hagar her _____ the Egyptian, after Abram had

dwelt ten years in the land of Canaan, and _____ her to her husband Abram

to be his wife. And he went in unto Hagar, and she _____: and when she

saw that she had conceived, her mistress was _____ in her eyes."

She obeyed the command of her mistress,
but was dealt with hardly by her.

Genesis 16:6

"But Abram said unto _____, Behold, thy maid is in thy _____;

do to her as it _____ thee. And when Sarai dealt _____ with her,

she fled from her face."

SHE WAS MET BY THE ANGEL OF THE LORD
AT A FOUNTAIN IN THE WILDERNESS.

The angel persuaded her to return to Sarai for the birth of her son.

Genesis 16:11-12

"And the _____ of the LORD said unto her, Behold, thou art with _____, and shalt bear a _____, and shalt call his name _____; because the LORD hath heard thy _____. And he will be a _____ man; his hand will be _____ every man, and every man's hand _____ him; and he shall dwell in the _____ of all his brethren."

SHE RETURNED TO GIVE BIRTH TO ISHMAEL.

Genesis 16:15-16

"And Hagar _____ Abram a son: and Abram called his son's _____, which Hagar bare, Ishmael. And Abram was _____ and six years old, when _____ bare Ishmael to Abram."

Sarai had been promised a son,
yet because of her impatience and doubt, she took matters into her own hands,
and went against what God had planned and promised.
Later, we will see more of the results of her disobedience.

She...

HAGAR SERVES AS AN EXAMPLE THAT WE CANNOT AVOID THE CONSEQUENCES OF OUR SINS.

Memorize:

Galatians 6:7
"Be not deceived; God is not mocked:
for whatsoever a man soweth, that shall he also reap."

Apply:

Why did Hagar flee from the face of Sarai?

_____

_____

Notes

_____

_____

_____

_____

_____

_____

_____

_____

_____

_____

_____

Herodias

Herodias

"...she could not:"

SHE WAS ONE OF THE MOST WICKED WOMEN.

Mark 6:17-18

*"For _____ himself had sent forth and laid hold upon John,
and bound him in prison for _____' sake, his brother Philip's wife:
for he had _____ her. For John had said unto Herod,
It is not _____ for thee to have thy brother's _____."*

John the Baptist called out Herod for their sin together.

Mark 6:19

"Therefore Herodias had a _____ against him,

and would have _____ him; but she could not:"

SHE PLOTTED AGAINST HIM, EVEN THOUGH HEROD FEARED HIM.

Mark 6:20

"For Herod feared John, knowing that he was a _____ man and an _____,

and _____ him; and when he heard him,

he did _____ things, and heard him gladly."

SHE HATED THE MAN OF GOD FOR EXPOSING HER SIN.

She used her daughter to manipulate Herod.

Mark 6:22

"And when the _____ of the said Herodias came in, and _____, and

pleased Herod and them that sat with him, the _____ said unto the damsel,

Ask of _____ whatsoever thou wilt, and I will _____ it thee."

She told her daughter to ask for John's head.

Mark 6:24

"And she went forth, and said unto her _____, What shall I _____?

And she said, The _____ of John the Baptist."

SHE EVENTUALLY GOT WHAT SHE WANTED.

Mark 6:27-28

"And immediately the king sent an _____, and commanded his head

to be brought: and he went and _____ him in the prison,

And brought his head in a _____, and gave it to the damsel:

and the damsel gave it to her _____."

SHE MURDERED A MAN OF GOD,
AND HAS BEEN CALLED THE JEZEBEL OF THE NEW TESTAMENT.

Sin has its consequences.

She...

HERODIAS SERVES AS AN EXAMPLE OF
THE DISGRACE THAT LUST AND SIN BRINGS
TO A LIFE CONSUMED WITH PRIDE.

Memorize:
James 1:15
"Then when lust hath conceived, it bringeth forth sin:
and sin, when it is finished, bringeth forth death."

Apply:
How can we avoid a life consumed with pride?

_____

_____

Notes

_____

_____

_____

_____

_____

_____

_____

_____

_____

_____

_____

Lot's Wife

Lot's Wife

Genesis 19:26

"...she became a pillar of salt."

SHE IS NOT NAMED WITHIN THE SCRIPTURES.

Her husband, Lot, met and married her within the cesspool fo Sodom,
and it was only because of his righteousness
that they were to be saved from the destruction.

Genesis 19:17

"And it came to pass, when they had brought them _____ abroad,

that he said, _____ for thy life; look not _____ thee,

neither stay thou in all the _____; escape to the mountain,

lest thou be _____."

The instructions were simple, yet she disobeyed.

Genesis 19:26

"But his wife _____ back from behind him,

and she became a _____ of salt."

SHE COULD HAVE BEEN SAVED.

However, her disobedience was a rejection of the salvation the Lord provided.

Jesus Christ spoke the only three words about her
to be recorded in the New Testament.

Luke 17:32

"*_____ Lot's wife.*"

SHE LIVED IN PLEASURE, BUT DIED IN HER SIN.

The Lord made a way for not only her life to be saved, but also a new life to begin.
Instead, one look of disobedience led to her grave.

SHE HEARD THE WORD OF GOD,
BUT DID NOT HEED TO HIS COMMAND.

She...

LOT'S WIFE SERVES AS AN EXAMPLE

THAT SIN HAS CONSEQUENCES.

If we choose to reject the salvation that the Lord has given us,
we too will become a pillar of regret.

Memorize:
Luke 17:33
*"Whosoever shall seek to save his life shall lose it;
and whosoever shall lose his life shall preserve it."*

Apply:
How have you learned from your own disobedience in the past?

_____

_____

_____

Notes

_____

_____

_____

_____

_____

_____

_____

_____

_____

_____

_____

Miriam

Miriam

"...she was leprous."

SHE WAS MOSES AND AARON'S SISTER.

SHE WAS A LEADER.

She is called a prophetess and led the women of Israel in praising the Lord
for His deliverance through the Red Sea.

Exodus 15:20-21

"And Miriam the _____, the sister of Aaron, took a timbrel in her hand;

and _____ the women went out after her with _____ and with dances.

And Miriam answered them, _____ ye to the LORD, for he hath triumphed

_____; the horse and his rider hath he thrown into the sea."

SHE LATER BECAME A LEADER OF DISCORD.

She and her brother, Aaron, spoke out against Moses
because of who he had married.

Numbers 12:1-2

"And Miriam and Aaron spake _____ Moses because of the Ethiopian woman

whom he had married: for he had married an _____ woman.

And they said, Hath the LORD indeed spoken _____ by Moses?

hath he not spoken _____ by us? And the LORD heard it."

Jealousy had consumed her.

She instigated Aaron to join her displeasure
of Moses' decision in marrying the Ethiopian woman.

The Lord sees and hears everything, and this was no different.
His wrath was kindled because of their indignation.

Numbers 12:9-10

"And the _____ of the LORD was kindled against them; and he departed.

And the _____ departed from off the tabernacle; and, behold,

Miriam became leprous, white as _____: and Aaron looked upon Miriam,

and, behold, she was _____."

Miriam received the judgment of God's wrath for their behavior.

Though Moses and Aaron pleaded with the Lord to have mercy upon her,
she was shut out of the camp for seven days, but was afterwards received in again.

SHE DID NOT SIN AGAINST MOSES; SHE SINNED AGAINST THE LORD BY REBELLING AGAINST HIS AUTHORITY.

She...

MIRIAM SERVES AS AN EXAMPLE THAT WHEN WE SIN AGAINST GOD THERE ARE CONSEQUENCES THAT WE CANNOT AVOID.

Memorize:
Numbers 32:23
"But if ye will not do so, behold, ye have sinned against the LORD:
and be sure your sin will find you out."

Apply:
How have you witnessed the evidence of God's judgment before?

_____

_____

_____

Notes

_____

_____

_____

_____

_____

_____

_____

_____

_____

_____

_____

Rebekah

Genesis 24:14

"...she that thou hast appointed..."

Genesis 24:14

"And let it come to pass, that the _____ to whom I shall say,

Let down thy _____, I pray thee, that I may drink; and she shall say,

Drink, and I will give thy _____ drink also: let the same be she that thou

hast appointed for thy servant _____; and thereby shall I know that thou

hast shewed _____ unto my master."

SHE WAS APPOINTED BY THE LORD FOR A SPECIFIC PURPOSE.

The servant begged the Lord to show him who the woman
was that He had chosen to be Isaac's wife.
The servant prayed, and the Lord answered.

Genesis 24:15

"And it came to pass, before he had _____ speaking, that,

behold, _____ came out, who was born to Bethuel, son of Milcah,

the wife of Nahor, Abraham's _____, with her pitcher upon her shoulder."

SHE WAS PREPARED
FOR WHAT GOD HAD PLANNED FOR HER.

Genesis 24:16-17

"And the damsel was very _____ to look upon, a virgin, neither had any man

known her: and she went down to the _____, and filled her pitcher, and came up.

And the servant ran to _____ her, and said,

Let me, I pray thee, drink a little _____ of thy pitcher."

SHE WAS OF THE KINDRED OF ABRAHAM,
JUST AS HE REQUESTED OF HIS SERVANT.

God answered his prayer for direction and provision.

She...

REBEKAH SERVES AS AN EXAMPLE THAT THE LORD

HAS A PURPOSE APPOINTED JUST FOR US.

We need only seek to yield to Him to bring us
to the people and places He has for us.

Memorize:

Psalm 32:8
*"I will instruct thee and teach thee in the way which thou shalt go:
I will guide thee with mine eye."*

Apply:

How has the Lord directed you before?

_____

_____

_____

Rebekah

"...she said, I will go"

SHE WAS WILLING TO GO
WHERE THE LORD WAS LEADING HER.

When she gave Abraham's servant and his camels drink,
she was ignorant of the significance of her actions.
She simply did what she was led to do,
unaware that what she did was an answer to someone else's prayer.

Genesis 24:45

"And before I had done speaking in mine _____, behold,

Rebekah came forth with her _____ on her shoulder; and she went down unto

the well, and drew water: and I said unto her, Let me drink, I _____ thee."

The servant came to her mother's house where her brother, Laban, greeted
him. After he came in, he began to tell the family the details of how he met
Rebekah at the well, and the importance of his quest to find her.
He praised the Lord for His direction,
then asked the family to oblige him taking her back to his master.

Genesis 24:48-49

"And I bowed down my head, and _____ the LORD, and blessed the LORD

God of my master Abraham, which had _____ me in the right way to take my

master's brother's daughter unto his _____. And now if ye will deal

_____ and truly with my master, tell me: and if not, tell me;

that I may _____ to the right hand, or to the left."

Their response was favorable, but they requested that she stay with them a
certain number of days before she went. The servant began to plead with them
that they must return now.

The family gave Rebekah the choice.

SHE WAS WILLING TO GO.

Genesis 24:58

"And they called _____, and said unto her,

Wilt _____ go with this man? And she said, I _____ go."

**Many blessings awaited her because of her willingness
to do what the Lord had purposed for her.**

Genesis 24:60

"And they _____ Rebekah, and said unto her, Thou art our sister,

be thou the _____ of thousands of millions,

and let thy _____ possess the gate of those which hate them."

She...

REBEKAH ALSO SERVES AS AN EXAMPLE OF WHAT CAN BE FOUND WHEN WE ARE WILLING TO GO WHERE THE LORD DIRECTS.

Our willingness to go shows our love for Him.

Memorize:

Isaiah 6:8
"Also I heard the voice of the Lord, saying, Whom shall I send,
and who will go for us? Then said I, Here am I; send me."

Apply:

Where is the Lord directing you to go?

_____

_____

Genesis 24:64

"...she saw Isaac..."

SHE SAW THE MAN THAT GOD HAD MADE FOR HER.

Genesis 24:64

"And Rebekah lifted up her _____,

and when she saw Isaac, she _____ off the camel."

SHE WAS BEAUTIFUL, YET MODEST.

Genesis 24:65

"For she had said unto the _____,

What _____ is this that walketh in the _____ to meet us?

And the servant had said, It is my _____:

therefore she took a _____, and _____ herself."

When she realized that her soon to be husband saw her,
she covered herself. Modesty is not overrated.

SHE BECAME THE WIFE OF ISAAC,
THE PROMISED SEED OF ABRAHAM.

Genesis 24:66-67

"And the servant told Isaac all _____ that he had done.

And Isaac brought her into his mother Sarah's _____, and took Rebekah,

and she _____ his wife; and he _____ her:

and Isaac was _____ after his mother's death."

SHE WAS LOVED BY ISAAC.

So much so, that her presence comforted him after his mother, Sarah, died.

If you are waiting for a husband, allow Rebekah's story to comfort you as you wait on the Lord to provide according to His will.

She...

REBEKAH ALSO SERVES AS AN EXAMPLE THAT GOD CAN HAND PICK OUR SPOUSE FOR US, AND THEN UNITE US WITH THEM THROUGH HIS DIVINE PROVIDENCE.

Memorize:

Psalm 27:14
*"Wait on the LORD: be of good courage,
and he shall strengthen thine heart: wait, I say, on the LORD."*

Apply:

Imagine how Rebekah must have felt when she saw Isaac... perhaps she remembered:

Genesis 24:60
*"... be thou the mother of thousands of millions,
and let thy seed possess the gate of those which hate them."*

How does that encourage you to follow the Lord's direction?

_____

_____

_____

Genesis 25:21

"...she was barren..."

SHE WAS BARREN OF A CHILD FOR TWENTY YEARS,
BUT WAS GIVEN CHILDREN BECAUSE SOMEONE PRAYED.

Genesis 25:21

"And Isaac _____ the LORD _____ his wife, because she was barren:

and the LORD was intreated of him, and Rebekah his wife _____."

Her husband prayed to the Lord on his wife's behalf.

Isaac desired they have a child,
and the Lord provided exceeding abundantly above what he asked.

SHE DID NOT HAVE AN EASY PREGNANCY.

Genesis 25:22

"And the children _____ together within her; and she said,

If it be so, _____ am I thus? And she went to _____ of the LORD."

**She asked the Lord to speak to her regarding her situation,
and He clearly did.**

Genesis 25:23

"And the LORD said unto her, _____ nations are in thy womb,

and two _____ of people shall be separated from thy bowels;

and the one people shall be _____ than the other people;

and the elder shall _____ the younger."

SHE DELIVERED TWIN BOYS
WHO COULD NOT BE MORE DIFFERENT.

Esau and Jacob were given after intercessory prayer was offered.
What a picture of how the Lord answers the cry of His people.

SHE WAS ONCE BARREN, BUT ENDED UP DOUBLY BLESSED.

When we have a need, He can provide even more than was asked.

Genesis 25:24-27

"And when her days to be delivered were _____, behold, there were _____ in her womb. And the first came out _____, all over like an hairy garment; and they called his name _____. And after that came his brother out, and his _____ took hold on Esau's _____; and his name was called _____: and Isaac was _____ years old when she bare them. And the boys grew: and Esau was a cunning _____, a man of the field; and Jacob was a _____ man, dwelling in tents."

She...

REBEKAH ALSO SERVES AS AN EXAMPLE THAT WHEN WE FEEL BARREN, GOD CAN INTERVENE.

Memorize:
Ephesians 3:20
"Now unto him that is able to do exceeding abundantly above all that we ask or think, according to the power that worketh in us,"

Apply:

How did Rebekah go from barren to doubly blessed?

_____

Notes

_____

_____

_____

_____

_____

_____

_____

_____

_____

_____

_____

Sarah

Genesis 11:30

"...she had no child."

SHE WAS ABRAM'S WIFE.

Genesis 11:29

"And _____ and Nahor took them wives:

the name of Abram's wife was _____;"

SHE WAS BARREN.

Genesis 11:30

"But Sarai was _____; she had no child."

SHE FOLLOWED HER HUSBAND.

She and her husband went forth with a few relatives
from Ur of the Chaldees toward the land of Canaan.

Then God commanded that they get out of their country,
away from their relatives, and into a land they had never seen.

Genesis 12:1

"Now the _____ had said unto Abram,

Get thee out of thy _____,

and from thy _____, and from thy father's house,

unto a _____ that I will shew thee:"

SHE HAD FAITH TO FOLLOW.

SHE FOLLOWED THE MAN SHE LOVED INTO A NEW LAND.

God gave them a great promise of what He would do through them.

Genesis 12:2-3

"And I will make of thee a _____ nation, and I will _____ thee,

and make thy _____ great; and thou _____ be a blessing:

And I will bless them that _____ thee, and curse him that _____ thee:

and in thee shall all _____ of the earth be blessed."

SHE MUST HAVE BEEN CONFUSED AT FIRST.

Her husband was promised a great nation of people, yet she had no child.

Genesis 12:7

"And the LORD _____ unto Abram, and said,

Unto thy _____ will I give this land: and there builded

he an _____ unto the LORD, who appeared unto him."

She...

SARAH SERVES AS AN EXAMPLE THAT GOD KEEPS HIS PROMISES.

Although it may not make sense to us, or even seem possible at the time, if He says it, He will do it.

Memorize:
Genesis 18:14
"Is any thing too hard for the LORD? At the time appointed I will return unto thee, according to the time of life, and Sarah shall have a son."

Apply:

What seems impossible to you right now?

_____
Ask the Lord to help you have faith in Him today.

Genesis 16:1

"...she had an handmaid..."

She was considered barren, yet she knew what God had promised.

Genesis 16:1

"Now Sarai Abram's wife bare him _____ children:

and she had an handmaid, an Egyptian, whose name was _____."

Why had she not gotten pregnant yet?
She was getting up in years,
and it seemed as if time was short.

She had an idea, and took matters into her own hands.

Genesis 16:2-4

"And Sarai said unto Abram, Behold now, the LORD hath _____ me

from bearing: I pray thee, go in unto my _____; it may be

that I may _____ children by her.

And Abram _____ to the voice of Sarai.

And Sarai Abram's wife took _____ her maid the Egyptian,

after Abram had dwelt ten years in the land of Canaan,

and gave her to her husband _____ to be his wife.

And he went in unto Hagar, and she _____:

and when she _____ that she had conceived,

her _____ was despised in her eyes."

She soon regretted her decision.

Genesis 16:5

"And Sarai said unto Abram, My _____ be upon thee:

I have _____ my maid into thy bosom;

and when she _____ that she had conceived,

I was _____ in her eyes: the LORD judge between me and thee."

SHE KNEW THERE WOULD BE CONSEQUENCES
FOR HER ACTIONS.

She...

SARAH ALSO SERVES AS AN EXAMPLE THAT
IT IS NOT WISE TO MANIPULATE SITUATIONS
TO FIT GOD'S PLAN FOR OUR LIVES.

His thoughts are higher than ours, and His ways are always better.

Memorize:

Isaiah 55:8-9

"For my thoughts are not your thoughts, neither are your ways my ways, saith the LORD.
For as the heavens are higher than the earth, so are my ways higher than your ways, and my thoughts than your thoughts."

Apply:

Why should we never manipulate the things that God has planned?

_____

_____

Genesis 17:16

"...she shall be a mother of nations..."

SHE HAD HER NAME CHANGED BY GOD BEFORE SHE RECEIVED THE PROMISED CHILD.

Genesis 17:15

"And God said unto Abraham, As for _____ thy wife,

thou shalt not call her _____ Sarai,

but _____ shall her name be."

God also changed her husband Abram's name to Abraham.

When God changes the name of one of His children,
it is for a distinct and special purpose that He is working within their lives.

SHE WAS PROMISED TO BE A MOTHER OF NOT JUST A SON, BUT OF NATIONS.

Genesis 17:16-17

"And I will bless her, and give thee a _____ also of her:

yea, I will _____ her, and she shall be a mother of nations;

kings of _____ shall be of her. Then Abraham fell upon his face,

and _____, and said in his heart,

Shall a child be _____ unto him that is an _____ years old?

and shall Sarah, that is _____ years old, bear?"

SHE WAS NINETY YEARS OLD.

Her husband was one hundred years old.
Both of them laughed when they were told what God had promised.

Genesis 17:19

"And God said, Sarah thy wife shall bear thee a son _____;

and thou shalt call his name _____: and I will establish

my covenant with him for an _____ covenant, and with his seed after him."

THEY BOTH DOUBTED THAT GOD COULD DO THE IMPOSSIBLE.

Genesis 18:11-12

"Now Abraham and Sarah were _____ and well stricken in age;

and it ceased to be with Sarah after the _____ of women.

Therefore Sarah _____ within herself, saying, After I am waxed old

shall I have pleasure, my lord being _____ also?"

Within the laughter, God saw there was doubt.

She...

SARAH ALSO SERVES AS AN EXAMPLE THAT THERE IS NOTHING TOO HARD FOR THE LORD.

**If He can provide the impossible for Sarah,
He is also able to do so for us.**

Memorize:

Jeremiah 32:17
"Ah Lord GOD! behold, thou hast made the heaven and the earth by thy great power and stretched out arm, and there is nothing too hard for thee:"

Apply:

How have you doubted God before?

_____

Genesis 18:15

"...she was afraid..."

Genesis 18:13-14

"And the LORD said unto _____, Wherefore did Sarah laugh,

saying, Shall I of a _____ bear a child, which am old?

Is any thing _____ hard for the LORD? At the time _____ I will return

unto thee, according to the _____ of life, and Sarah _____ have a son."

She lied out of fear.

Genesis 18:15

"Then Sarah _____, saying, I laughed not; for she was afraid.

And he said, _____; but thou didst laugh."

The Lord sees and hears our doubtful hearts.

She had to wait.

She did not know when she would have a son.
Abraham was 86 when Ishmael was born.
They waited 14 years for Isaac.

The longer she waited, the more of a miracle her situation became.

Genesis 21:1-3

"And the LORD _____ Sarah as he had said, and the LORD _____ unto Sarah

as he had spoken. For Sarah _____, and bare Abraham a _____ in his

old age, at the _____ time of which God had _____ to him. And Abraham

called the _____ of his son that was _____ unto him,

whom Sarah bare to him, _____."

Even in their old age, God provided the child He had promised.

Isaiah 64:4

"For since the _____ of the world men have not heard,

nor perceived by the_____, neither hath the _____ seen,

O God, beside thee, what he hath _____ for him that waiteth for him."

Waiting sometimes causes us to fear the unknown.
There is no need to fear when we trust in Him.

She...

SARAH ALSO SERVES AS AN EXAMPLE THAT WHEN WAITING MAKES US FEARFUL, GOD ALWAYS HAS A PLAN.

Memorize:
Psalm 56:3
"What time I am afraid, I will trust in thee."

Apply:

What did Abraham and Sarah do when God told them they would have a child in old age?

_____

When have you been afraid of the unknown?

_____

Sarah

Hebrews 11:11

"...she judged him faithful who had promised."

SHE HAD FAITH.

Even though she laughed, even though she was afraid,
she is still known for her faith.

SHE IS ONE OF ONLY TWO WOMEN MENTIONED IN HEBREWS 11.

Hebrews 11:11-12

"Through _____ also Sara herself received _____ to conceive seed,

and was delivered of a child when she was _____ age, because she judged

him faithful who had promised. _____ sprang there even of one,

and him as good as dead, so many as the _____ of the sky in multitude,

and as the _____ which is by the sea shore innumerable."

SHE GAVE BIRTH TO ISAAC IN HER OLD AGE.

He was the promised seed, and the only child of Abraham's that God recognized.

Genesis 22:2

"And he said, Take now thy son, thine _____ son Isaac,

whom thou _____, and get thee into the land of Moriah;

and _____ him there for a burnt offering upon one of the mountains

which I will _____ thee of."

The Scripture is silent on where Sarah was or if she even knew about her
husband taking their son up Mount Moriah to offer him as a burnt offering.

Can you imagine how she must have felt if she knew?

The last time she is mentioned beforehand she tells Abraham
to cast out Hagar after Sarah sees Ishmael mocking Isaac.

The next time she is mentioned, she has died.

Genesis 23:1-2

"And Sarah was an _____ and seven and twenty years old:

these were the years of the life of Sarah. And Sarah _____ in Kirjatharba;

the same is Hebron in the land of Canaan: and Abraham came to _____ for

Sarah, and to _____ for her."

Regardless of how much Sarah did or did not know
about the offering of her son, her faith shined through her life.

**Every time she looked at her son, she was reminded that
God is Faithful to keep His promises.**

She...

SARAH ALSO SERVES AS AN EXAMPLE THAT GOD IS FAITHFUL.

His faithfulness should encourage us to stay faithful to Him.

Memorize:

Hebrews 10:23
*"Let us hold fast the profession of our faith without wavering;
(for he is faithful that promised;)"*

Apply:

Why is Sarah included in the Hall of Faith in Hebrews 11?

_____

See Hebrews 11:11.

Notes

_____

_____

_____

_____

_____

_____

_____

_____

_____

_____

_____

The Maid By The Fire

The Maid By The Fire

Mark 14:67

"...she looked upon him..."

Up above the fire, Jesus stood before the High Priest.

Mark 14:66

"And as Peter was _____ in the palace,

there cometh one of the _____ of the high priest:"

SHE RECOGNIZED PETER.

Mark 14:67

"And when she saw Peter _____ himself,

she looked upon him, and said, And thou also wast with _____ of Nazareth."

Luke 22:56

"But a certain _____ beheld him as he sat by the _____,

and earnestly _____ upon him, and said,

This _____ was also with him."

John 18:17

"Then saith the _____ that kept the door unto Peter,

Art not thou also one of this man's _____?

He saith, I am _____."

SHE HEARD PETER DENY CHRIST.

Mark 14:68

"But he _____, saying, I know not,

neither _____ I what thou sayest.

And he went _____ into the porch; and the cock crew."

SHE MUST HAVE HEARD THE COCK CROW.

Mark 14:72

"And the _____ time the cock crew.

And Peter called to mind the word that _____ said unto him,

Before the cock crow _____, thou shalt deny me thrice.

And when he thought thereon, he _____."

Would others be able to say that we have been with Jesus?

She...

THE MAID BY THE FIRE SERVES AS AN EXAMPLE OF HOW PEOPLE ARE WATCHING OUR TESTIMONY.

Memorize:

1 Timothy 4:12
"Let no man despise thy youth; but be thou an example of the believers, in word, in conversation, in charity, in spirit, in faith, in purity."

Apply:

How many times did Peter deny Christ?

_____

How many times did the cock crow?

_____

Notes

_____

_____

_____

_____

_____

_____

_____

_____

_____

_____

The Queen Of Sheba

The Queen Of Sheba

1 Kings 10:1

"...she came to prove him with hard questions."

1 Kings 10:1

"And when the queen of Sheba heard of the fame of _____

concerning the _____ of the LORD, she came to prove him with hard questions."

SHE SOUGHT HIS WISDOM.

1 Kings 10:2

"And she came to _____ with a very great train, with camels that bare spices,

and very much gold, and precious stones: and when she was _____ to Solomon,

she _____ with him of all that was in her heart."

SHE WAS CURIOUS
IF WHAT SHE HAD HEARD WAS TRUE.

1 Kings 10:3

"And Solomon told her _____ her questions: there was not _____ thing hid

from the king, which he _____ her not."

SHE WAS ASTOUNDED AT HIS WISDOM AND WEALTH.

1 Kings 10:4-5

"And when the queen of Sheba had seen all Solomon's _____, and the house

that he had _____, And the meat of his table, and the sitting of his _____

and the attendance of his ministers, and their apparel, and his _____,

and his ascent by which he went up unto the _____ of the LORD;

there was no more _____ in her."

SHE FOUND WHAT SHE HAD HEARD WAS TRUE.

1 Kings 10:6

"And she said to the king, It was a true _____ that I heard

in mine own land of thy _____ and of thy _____."

Jesus Christ referred to her when certain of the scribes
and Pharisees asked for a sign from Him.

Matthew 12:42

"The queen of the _____ shall rise up in the judgment with this generation,

and shall condemn it: for she came from the _____ parts of the earth to

hear the wisdom of Solomon; and, behold, a _____ than Solomon is here."

She...

THE QUEEN OF SHEBA SERVES AS AN EXAMPLE THAT WHEN WE SEEK THE LORD, WE ARE CERTAIN TO FIND HIM AND MUCH MORE.

Memorize:

James 1:5-6

"If any of you lack wisdom, let him ask of God, that giveth to all men liberally, and upbraideth not; and it shall be given him. But let him ask in faith, nothing wavering. For he that wavereth is like a wave of the sea driven with the wind and tossed."

Apply:

How can we receive wisdom?

_____

Notes

_____

_____

_____

_____

_____

_____

_____

_____

_____

_____

The Widow With Oil

The Widow With Oil

2 Kings 4:5

> "...she poured out."

SHE OWED A GREAT DEBT.

2 Kings 4:1

"Now there cried a certain _____ of the wives of the sons of the prophets unto Elisha, saying, Thy servant my _____ is dead; and thou knowest that thy servant did fear the LORD: and the _____ is come to take unto him my two sons to be _____."

SHE KNEW WHERE TO GO FOR HELP.

2 Kings 4:2

"And Elisha said unto her, What shall I _____ for thee? tell me, what hast thou in the_____? And she said, Thine handmaid hath not _____ thing in the house, save a _____ of oil."

Elisha told her to do something illogical.

2 Kings 4:3-4

"Then he said, Go, borrow thee _____ abroad of all thy neighbours, even empty vessels; borrow _____ a few. And when thou art come in thou shalt shut the door upon thee and upon thy sons, and shalt _____ out into all those vessels, and thou shalt set aside that which is _____."

SHE CHOSE TO OBEY WHAT THE MAN OF GOD SAID.

2 Kings 4:5

"So she went from him, and _____ the door upon her and upon her sons, who brought the _____ to her; and she poured out."

| 89

2 Kings 4:6

"And it came to pass, when the vessels were _____, that she said unto her son,

Bring me _____ a vessel. And he said unto her, There is not a vessel more.

And the oil _____."

The oil stayed because she had faith.
God provided a solution to her problem.

SHE SAW THE LORD PROVIDE EXACTLY WHAT SHE NEEDED.

2 Kings 4:7

"Then she came and told the man of God. And he said, Go, _____ the oil,

and _____ thy debt, and _____ thou and thy children of the rest."

Where God guides, He provides.

She...

THE WIDOW WITH OIL SERVES AS AN EXAMPLE OF HOW GOD CAN PROVIDE EXACTLY WHAT WE NEED.

Memorize:

Isaiah 58:11
"And the LORD shall guide thee continually, and satisfy thy soul in drought, and make fat thy bones: and thou shalt be like a watered garden, and like a spring of water, whose waters fail not."

Apply:

How has the Lord provided for you before?

_____

_____

Notes

_____

_____

_____

_____

_____

_____

_____

_____

_____

_____

_____

The Woman With A Spirit Of Infirmity

The Woman With A Spirit Of Infirmity

Read: Luke 13:10-17   Luke 13:13

"...she was made straight, and glorified God."

SHE WAS BOWED TOGETHER.

Luke 13:11

"And, behold, there was a _____ which had a spirit of infirmity

_____ years, and was bowed together,

and could in no wise _____ up herself."

SHE WAS HELPLESS.

For eighteen years she had suffered at the hand of Satan, until she met Jesus.

Luke 13:12

"And when _____ saw her,

he _____ her to him, and said unto her,

Woman, thou art _____ from thine infirmity."

SHE WAS HEALED.

Luke 13:13

"And he laid his _____ on her:

and _____ she was made straight,

and _____ God."

After Jesus spoke to her, she was never the same.

Luke 13:16

"And ought not this woman, being a _____ of Abraham,

whom Satan hath _____, lo, these eighteen years,

be loosed from this _____ on the sabbath day?"

She...

THE WOMAN WITH A SPIRIT OF INFIRMITY SERVES AS AN EXAMPLE OF WHAT CHRIST HAS BROUGHT US FROM.

We were all bound in sin before we met Him.

Memorize:

Romans 5:20
"Moreover the law entered, that the offence might abound. But where sin abounded, grace did much more abound:"

Apply:

How many years was she bowed together?

_____

How can we be loosed from our sin?

_____

_____

_____

Notes

_____

_____

_____

_____

_____

_____

_____

_____

_____

_____

Be A Woman Of The Bible

Be A Woman Of The Bible

Did you know that there are three distinct ways to understand the Bible?

Read
Deuteronomy 17:19

Search
John 5:39

Study
2 Timothy 2:15

You have studied the lives of 12 Women of the Bible.
Their names or testimonies are recorded on the pages of the Word of God for specific purposes. The characteristics of their lives are examples of the many things you can choose to apply to your life.

Although your name is not printed in the canon of the Scriptures, you can still be known as a Woman of the Bible by purposing yourself to use the qualities of their lives to affect how you walk with the Lord.

The Book of James describes two different choices you have
in your response to what you find in the Word of God.

James 1:22-25
"But be ye doers of the word, and not hearers only, deceiving your own selves.
For if any be a hearer of the word, and not a doer, he is like unto a man beholding his
natural face in a glass: For he beholdeth himself, and goeth his way,
and straightway forgetteth what manner of man he was.
But whoso looketh into the perfect law of liberty, and continueth therein, he being
not a forgetful hearer, but a doer of the work, this man shall be blessed in his deed."

LIVE OUT WHAT YOU KNOW.

If you are to be known as a woman who follows Biblical Truth,
you have to live out what you know.
"doers of the word, and not hearers only"

There is a difference between what you know and what you believe.

Many people who call themselves "Christians" know Biblical Truth.
They know that Jesus Christ was the Son of God.
They know that Jesus died on the cross.

They even know that He died on the cross of their sins.
They know a lot of things...but have they believed on Him?

**There is a difference in knowing something,
and actually believing, or placing your faith in it.**

Many have heard the phrase that "people can be 18 inches away from Heaven".
The principle found here is so true.

Many know that Abraham Lincoln was the 16th President of the United States of America. Many even know that he famously spoke the Emancipation Proclamation, and that he led the abolishment of slavery.

They have never met him, yet they know many things about him.

There are many people that know countless facts about Who Jesus is, yet they have not placed their faith and trust in what He did on the cross for them.

That is the difference.

LIVE OUT WHAT YOU BELIEVE.

The same principle applies to the women you have studied throughout this book. You can know everything about their lives, so much so that you could clear the "Women of the Bible" column on the Jeopardy board, but if you do not apply what you know to your life it simply ends with knowledge.

You can know many many things found within the pages of God's Word, but if you only hear them without being a doer of those Truths, the Book of James clearly says that you are deceiving yourself.

Be A Woman Of The Bible

References

References

DELILAH
"Delicate or Dainty One"

JUDGES 16:4-21

ESTHER
"A Star"

THE BOOK OF ESTHER

HAGAR
"Fugitive or Immigrant"

GENESIS 16; 21:9-17; 25:12; GALATIANS 4:24, 25

HERODIAS
"Heroic"

MATTHEW 14:3-12; MARK 6:14-24; LUKE 3:19, 20

LOT'S WIFE

GENESIS 19:15-26; LUKE 17:29-33

MIRIAM
"Bitterness or Rebellion"

EXODUS 15:20, 21; NUMBERS 12:1-15; 20:1; 26:59; DEUTERONOMY 24:9; MICAH 6:4

REBEKAH
"A Tie Rope for Animals or A Noose"

GENESIS 22:23; 24; 25:20-28; 26:6-35; 27; 28:5; 29:12; 35:8; 49:31; ROMANS 9:6-16

SARAH

Sarai: "Princely or A Princess"

Sarah: "Captain or Commander"

GENESIS 11:29-31; 12:5-17; 16:1-8; 17:15-21; 18; 20:2-18; 21:1-12; 23:1-19; 24:36-37; 25:10, 12; 49:31; ISAIAH 51:2; ROMANS 4:19; 9:9; HEBREWS 11:11-12; 1 PETER 3:6

THE MAID BY THE FIRE

MATTHEW 26:69-71; MARK 14:66-69; LUKE 22:56-59; JOHN 18:16-17

THE QUEEN OF SHEBA

1 KINGS 10:1-13; 2 CHRONICLES 9:1-12; MATTHEW 12:42

THE WIDOW WITH OIL

2 KINGS 4:1-7

THE WOMAN WITH A SPIRIT OF INFIRMITY

LUKE 13:11-13

About Us

About Us

"Delight thyself also in the LORD;
and he shall give thee the desires of thine heart."
Psalm 37:4

From this verse comes the inspiration behind the name of this ministry. It is a reminder that if we delight ourselves in Him, He promises to give us desires according to His will for our lives.

In 2012, the desire for a design ministry began. The Lord has since opened door after door to allow that desire to become a reality...*"Commit thy way unto the LORD; trust also in him; and he shall bring it to pass."* Psalm 37:5

Delight Thyself Design Ministries began as a media ministry at Teays Valley Baptist Church of Hurricane, WV. Then Lord directed us toward reaching people with the printed Word of the Gospel. A tract ministry was born, and has since continued to grow as the Lord leads. In 2014, we began shipping tracts to missionaries across the world with little or no material with which to reach their field. **Please pray with us** that the Lord will continue to provide resources to print the tracts the missionaries are requesting.

We ship tracts free of charge to anyone willing to distribute the printed Word of the Gospel of Jesus Christ. Contact us if you would like to receive a sample pack or box to distribute.

Gospel tracts customized with a church's contact information are a great way to spread the Gospel and allow others to contact your ministry. We also design custom material for Independent Baptist Churches, which helps fund the printing and distribution of Gospel tracts which are sent across the world.

We are so thankful for those whom the Lord has provided to support this ministry on a monthly basis or through one time donations. If it were not for the Lord using these generous people, this ministry simply could not exist today. We claim Philippians 4:17 for this method of support, *"Not because I desire a gift: but I desire fruit that may abound to your account."*

If you would like to receive ministry updates, follow us on social media or send us your email address to receive our newsletters.

Delight Thyself
DESIGN MINISTRIES

delightthyself.com

What Can One Tract Do?

One tract was sitting in the office of the home of a young man named, Hudson. When he found it, he read over it and the phrase "the finished work of Christ" began to work on his heart about his need for salvation. He then surrendered his life to Christ, and was burdened for the people of China. This man was who we now know as Hudson Taylor, the missionary who brought the Good News of the Gospel to China.

One tract was given by a friend to a man named Joe. Over the next several months, the Lord used that tract to put him under conviction, cause him to go to church and walk the aisle to trust Christ as His Saviour. When he got up, he saw his pregnant wife beside him. She had also came forward by faith to accept Christ. This is the testimony of the parents of the founder of this ministry. One tract led to their salvation, a Christian heritage, and the start of this ministry. Without God using a man to give that one tract, this ministry would not exist today.

One tract has now yielded nearly five million tracts to date being sent all across the world, and only heaven will reveal the fruit that remains. To God be the glory, for great things only He hath done.

Isaiah 55:11
"So shall my word be that goeth forth out of my mouth:
it shall not return unto me void,
but it shall accomplish that which I please,
and it shall prosper in the thing whereto I sent it."

Will you allow God to use you
to spread the printed Word of the Gospel?

Visit delightthyself.com for more resources.

ONE TRACT
CAN
MAKE A
DIFFERENCE

The Bible Way To Heaven

"Jesus saith unto him, I am the way, the truth, and the life:
no man cometh unto the Father, but by me."
John 14:6

We Are All Sinners.
"For all have sinned, and come short of the glory of God."
Romans 3:23

We Were Sent A Saviour.
"But God commendeth his love toward us, in that,
while we were yet sinners, Christ died for us."
Romans 5:8

We Were Supplied A Gift.
"For the wages of sin is death;
but the gift of God is eternal life through Jesus Christ our Lord."
Romans 6:23

We Can Simply Confess & Call.
"That if thou shalt confess with thy mouth the Lord Jesus,
and shalt believe in thine heart that God
hath raised him from the dead, thou shalt be saved.
For whosoever shall call upon the name of the Lord shall be saved."
Romans 10:9,13

It's that simple.

The Bible says... **Whosoever.**
Once you see yourself as a sinner, if you will simply *"call upon the name of the Lord"*, you can be saved from spending eternity in the Lake of Fire separated from God. You may say..."It's not for me." or "I'll never be good enough.", but God said... **Whosoever.**

God is not willing that any should perish.
That includes you.

If you have trusted Christ as your Saviour,
or would like more information, please contact us.

delightthyself.com

www.ingramcontent.com/pod-product-compliance
Lightning Source LLC
Chambersburg PA
CBHW041538120626
46551CB00019B/2749